Italy adopted its coat of arms when it became a republic in 1946. The laurel and oak branches represent republicanism, the star is for unity and the cog is for industry. The tricolour flag (top left) became the national flag in 1870. Designed by Napoléon in 1796 when he invaded Italy, it was inspired by the French flag, with green replacing the blue section.

The family
The family is very important to Italians. Most young Italians live with their parents until they marry, which may not be until they are in their late twenties or early thirties. A minority of single children do live away from home and this is on the increase. In the countryside it is still common for the extended family – uncles, aunts and cousins – to live under the same roof, or at least near to each other. This provides a framework in which very old and very young members of the family are taken care of. The national trend, however, is for families to become smaller. In the last twenty years the number of children per family has fallen to an average of just 1.2 – the world's lowest birth rate.

Traditional dress
Local, traditional costume is usually only worn for festivals. Costumes vary from region to region and even from village to village. In the Alto Adige, for instance, the Tyrolean costumes are influenced by bordering Austria; traditional Sardinian costume has Spanish elements, reflecting the island's past occupation by Spain.

Two women in traditional Tyrolean costume

Art and monuments
Italy is uniquely rich in art and historic buildings. According to UNESCO, two-thirds of the world's historical artistic heritage are in Italy, and Tuscany alone has more classical monuments than any other country in the world. Students of art have always tried to spend some time in Italy, be they painters, sculptors or architects. Italy's artistic tradition stretches as far back as the Romans and is still flourishing today.

ROMANS TO RENAISSANCE

The Romans united Italy under a single ruler. When the Roman Empire fell, Italy was invaded many times and was broken up into several smaller states. By 1200, much of Italy was divided between the Holy Roman Emperor and the Pope. Cities like Venice and Genoa had achieved near independence and grew rich from trading. This wealth and new ways of thinking sparked off the Renaissance, making Italy the cultural centre of Europe.

Date chart

900-500 BC Etruscans arrive in Italy from Asia Minor and Greece.

300-146 BC Rome defeats Carthage and becomes dominant in the western Mediterranean.

58-51 BC Julius Caesar (above centre) conquers Gaul.

27 BC Augustus (above left) becomes first emperor.

43 AD Romans invade Britain.

117 AD The Roman Empire is at its height but Emperor Hadrian (above right) limits further expansion.

285 AD The Empire is divided into Eastern and Western Empires.

330 AD Emperor Constantine makes Byzantium the Empire's capital, renamed Constantinople.

476 AD Last emperor, Romulus Augustus, is deposed. Italy is occupied by barbarian tribes. The Popes become powerful.

800 AD The Pope crowns Charlemagne Emperor of the Romans.

962 AD Italy becomes part of the Holy Roman Empire under Otto.

c.1000 AD Italian city states become important.

c.1300 AD Renaissance begins.

Roman Empire

With a stable government at home and a strong army, the Romans invaded much of Europe. At its peak, the Empire (right) stretched from Britain to Africa to the River Euphrates in Iraq. The Romans took many slaves and charged taxes, but left the alphabet, laws, roads, city planning and the arts, such as mosaics (left).

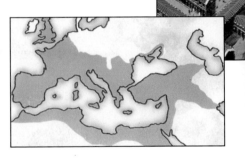

The Hollywood view

For centuries, tales of the Roman Empire have fascinated playwrights. In the 20th century, Hollywood has made many movies, such as *Ben Hur*, *Spartacus* and *Gladiator*, that depict life in ancient Rome. Although these movies romanticise Roman life, they do give us a feel for what life may have been like.

Science, technology and maths

The microscope symbol shows where a science or maths subject is included. If the symbol is tinted green, it signals an environmental issue. This includes a look at Galileo's discoveries and at conservation.

History

The sign of the scroll and the hourglass indicates where historical information is given. These sections look at key figures and events in Italian history and their influence today.

Social history

The symbol of the family shows where information about social history is given. These sections look at Italian lifestyle, religious beliefs, traditional festivals and customs.

Arts, crafts and music

The symbol showing a sheet of music and art tools signals where information on arts, crafts or music are included. This book features some of Italy's great artists, craftspeople and musicians.

CONTENTS

INTRODUCTION TO ITALY

Italy is the boot-shaped peninsula which, together with Sardinia, Sicily and some other smaller islands, stretches into the Mediterranean from southern Europe to within a few kilometres of the African coast. Bordered by France, Switzerland, Austria and Slovenia to the north, Italy covers an area of 301,225 km² and has a population of over 57 million. It has been a single country since 1870 and a republic, with an elected president as head of state, since 1946. Italy is one of the founder members of the European Union (see page 31) and has become one of Europe's most important economies.

(see page 31)

Language

Italian is a Romance language – it evolved from Latin, the language of the Romans. Standard Italian is the main language of most Italians. It is used in schools and by the media. It evolved from a dialect spoken in Tuscany. Many regions have their own dialect. These are often difficult for other Italians to understand. In border regions there are French, German and Slovene speakers. In Sardinia, 1.5 million people speak a language called Sard.

Galileo

Galileo Galilei (1564-1642) An astronomer, mathematician and inventor; Galileo has been called the founder of modern science. He made many discoveries, but his most important achievement was to confirm that the Earth revolved around the Sun. The Roman Catholic Church jailed him for this discovery, insisting that the Earth was the centre of the universe.

The Popes

The Roman Catholic Church gradually replaced the Roman Empire as the centre of authority in western Europe. By 1302, papal power had grown so much that the Pope claimed the right to depose heads of state. By the Renaissance, the papacy had become corrupt. It suffered a loss of power when it was forced to grant the English and French kings shares of church land and taxes in their countries.

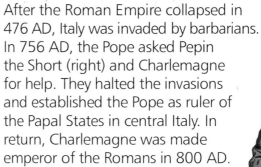

After the Roman Empire collapsed in 476 AD, Italy was invaded by barbarians. In 756 AD, the Pope asked Pepin the Short (right) and Charlemagne for help. They halted the invasions and established the Pope as ruler of the Papal States in central Italy. In return, Charlemagne was made emperor of the Romans in 800 AD.

Renaissance

The Renaissance began in Italy in the 14th century. It spread to western Europe and flourished until the 16th century. As the city states grew richer, wealthy families were keen to win prestige by sponsoring the arts. This period saw a revival of interest in classical Greek and Roman civilisation. Renaissance means rebirth, and it describes the sense of being reborn into the light of learning and knowledge after the chaos of centuries of invasions. The Renaissance was a time of great artistic achievement, free thinking and adventure. Practical inventions such as printing helped spread new ideas. It was a time of scientific advancement; voyages of discovery were made to Africa, Asia and the New World. The Renaissance is regarded as the end of the Middle Ages and the start of modern times.

The Byzantine Empire

By the 3rd century AD, Rome could no longer hold the Empire together. In 285 AD, the emperor Diocletian divided it into two parts – west and east. Invasions and inflation led to the collapse of the Western Empire. Constantine became emperor of the west in 306 AD. He reunited the two halves of the Empire and moved his court to Byzantium, renamed Constantinople. In 313 AD, he granted Christians freedom of worship. By 500 AD, a Byzantine style of art had developed and spread to many parts of Europe including Italy. Today, you can see 6th century Byzantine mosaics at San Vitale church in Ravenna (left).

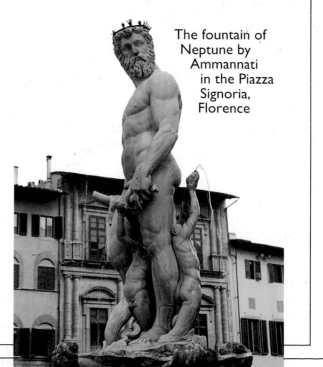

The fountain of Neptune by Ammannati in the Piazza Signoria, Florence

1500 TO TODAY

By the beginning of the 16th century, the wealth of the Italian city states had made them attractive to foreign invaders. For the next two centuries the peninsula suffered invasions by France, Austria and Spain. After Napoléon's invasion in 1796, there was a recognition that the states of Italy could be united as one country. In the 19th century, the struggle to achieve this began. In 1870, Italy became a unified kingdom. In the 20th century, after dictatorship and war, it became a democratic republic (see pages 20-21).

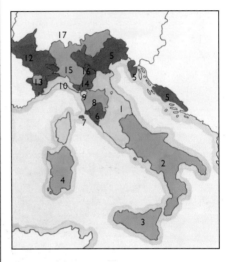

Italy c.1500
1 Papal states
2 Naples (Spain)
3 Sicily (Spain)
4 Sardinia (Spain)
5 Venice
6 Siena
7 Piombino
8 Florence
9 Lucca
10 Genoa
11 Asti
12 Savoy
13 Saluzzo
14 Modena
15 Milan
16 Mantua
17 Holy Roman Empire

Risorgimento

The Risorgimento was a movement to expel foreign powers from Italy and unite it as a single country. Nationwide uprisings in 1848 and 1849 failed, but Count Cavour, prime minister of Piedmont, enlisted French help to drive the Austrians out in 1861. Garibaldi conquered Sicily and Naples, and the Italian kingdom was founded in 1861, with the king of Sardinia, Victor Emmanuel II, as king. Unification was completed by 1871 with the addition of the Papal States, and Rome was made the capital.

Date chart
1519 Charles V of Spain becomes Holy Roman Emperor.
1521-59 Spain and Holy Roman Empire defeat France to control Italy.
1713 Austrian Habsburgs take over Northern Italy, other areas hang onto or gain independence.
1735 House of Bourbon takes over Naples and Sicily.
1768 Genoa sells Corsica to France.
1796 Napoléon invades.
1805 Napoléon's brother Joseph is made king of Naples.
1815 Congress of Vienna returns Italy to former rulers – once again a series of separate states.
1800s Risorgimento (process of unification) led by the House of Savoy.
1870 Italy united as single country, Victor Emmanuel II made king.

1915 Italy enters World War I.
1936 Mussolini forms alliance with Hitler.
1940 Italy enters World War II.
1943 Allies invade Italy.
1946 Italy becomes a republic.
1950 Italy a founder member of NATO.
1957 Italy signs Treaty of Rome.
1978 Former prime minister Aldo Moro murdered by terrorists.
1981 Pope shot at St. Peter's in Rome.
1994 Elections introduce new parties to parliament after years of corruption.
2002 Italy joins the European single currency, the euro.

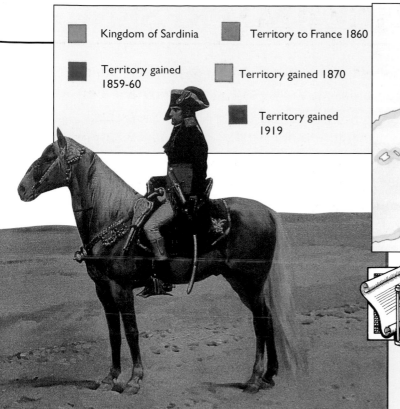

■ Kingdom of Sardinia	■ Territory to France 1860
■ Territory gained 1859-60	■ Territory gained 1870
	■ Territory gained 1919

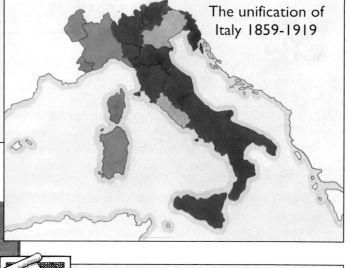

The unification of Italy 1859-1919

Napoléon

Napoléon invaded Italy in 1796 and, although his rule lasted less than 20 years, he had a profound influence. His system was harsh at times, and taxes were high, but laws, currency and the army were brought under a single administration. For the first time since the Romans, Italians saw the possibility of living in a united country, free from foreign control.

Italy at War

Italy entered World War I on the side of Britain and France in return for portions of land, including African territory, if they won. The war proved a waste of men and materials. In two years, Italy gained only 15km of land. At the end of the war, Italy gained less territory than was promised. In an effort to build a new empire, Mussolini invaded Ethiopia in 1935 and Albania in 1939. Italy entered World War II in support of Nazi Germany. But the Italian army was unprepared and lost every campaign. In 1943, the Allies landed. Italy surrendered, then fought with the Allies.

Benito Mussolini (1883-1945)

Mussolini founded the Fascist movement in 1919. Popular with landowners and industrialists, he also appealed to war veterans. In 1922, the Fascists marched on Rome and Mussolini was made prime minister. In 1925, he took the title Il Duce (leader) and became dictator. The Fascists used terror and propaganda to stop opposition, but were popular because they created jobs and rebuilt the army. Mussolini was defeated and shot at the end of World War II.

INFLUENCE AND PRESENCE

The Roman Empire and the Renaissance may be long gone, but the great civilising force of the Romans, and the cultural explosion of the Renaissance can still be felt today. Between 1850 and 1950, many Italians, particularly from the poorer south, emigrated to the Americas and elsewhere to escape poverty and political upheavals, taking their culture with them. One unappealing export was the Mafia, which has flourished, particularly in the United States (see page 18). Since 1945, northern Italy has become one of Europe's most advanced industrial areas. Its automotive and design industries are world leaders.

Roman town planning
Roman towns and cities were carefully planned. They were built on a grid pattern with public buildings conveniently located, and sewage and water systems provided. Cities are still planned according to the grid pattern today. The best example is New York, in the United States. Roman engineering made large buildings possible. They realised the potential of the arch for bridges, aqueducts, and vaulted roofs that eliminated the need for columns. They also invented concrete. In recent times, Italian engineers have acquired a reputation for ingenuity, particularly in the fields of road and railway construction.

Roman law
The Romans developed a unified system of law that became the basis for many legal systems in Western Europe and Latin America. Their first code of law, called the Laws of the Twelve Tables, was published around 450 BC. Roman law was flexible and depended on the interpretation of lawyers and judges. They developed a general set of legal principles for everyone who lived under Roman rule, called the law of nations. It was based on common sense and fairness. It spread throughout the Empire, and was adaptable enough for local practices and customs to be taken into account.

Writers

Italian literature has a long and distinguished history. The works of the Roman poet Virgil (70-19 BC) influenced many later writers. Based on his experiences as a diplomat, Nicoló Machiavelli (1469-1527) wrote *The Prince*, which advised leaders on the best way to achieve political success.

Italian style

Italians seem to know almost instinctively what looks good. They take great care in their appearance, and are perhaps the world's most elegant dressers. Italians typically spend a lot of money on clothes for themselves and their children; "made in Italy" tends to mean high quality. Many of the world's leading high fashion designers are Italian, such as Giorgio Armani (left) and Donatella Versace.

Accessories are important too, and Italy's shoes, bags and belts are among the best in the world. The Italian eye for good design goes beyond clothes. It reaches industries as diverse as computer manufacture to furniture design (below left). Italian cars, for both the road and the race track, have long been renowned for their sleek lines; and Italian architecture has influenced European tastes since Roman times.

Opera

Opera was born in Italy, pioneered by the composer Monteverdi in the early 17th century. Other famous composers followed, such as Rossini (*The Barber of Seville*), Verdi (*Rigoletto, La Traviata*) and Puccini (*Tosca, Madame Butterfly*). La Scala opera house in Milan and the tenor Luciano Pavarotti (below) are internationally famous, and opera is immensely popular. Italians are as familiar with opera as they are with pop songs.

Italian cuisine

One of the great imports by immigrant Italians to their adoptive countries was their cooking, now famous the world over. It is varied, full of flavour and healthy, often made from simple ingredients that are easy to find. Italian cuisine is recognised as one of the world's finest.

THE COUNTRY

Apart from the Po river plain in the north-east, Italy is dominated by two mountain ranges, the Alps in the north and the Apennines, which stretch down the centre of the peninsula like a backbone. Italy is surrounded by four seas: the Ligurian, Tyrrhenian, Ionian and Adriatic. There are two large islands: Sicily and Sardinia. Italy's climate is varied with cold winters and hot summers in the north and hot, dry summers and mild winters in the south.

Dolomites
Alps
Po Valley
Adriatic Plain
Ligurian Sea
Apennines
Western Uplands
Adriatic Sea
Sardinia
Tyrrhenian Sea
Ionian Sea
Sicily

Mountains
In Italy's Alpine region, you will find glaciers and deep lakes. The Alps' highest peak, Mont Blanc (4,807m), is on the French border. Parts of the Apennines are still volcanic and earthquakes can be a hazard.

Waterways and coastlines
Italy's longest river is the Po. It is 644km long and runs into the Adriatic. Other major rivers are the Adige and the Brenta. Italy's 7,400km of coastline includes sandy beaches and towering cliffs.

Countryside
The varied Italian countryside ranges from the Alpine north, to green and fertile plains, forested valleys, rolling fields and arid, rocky peaks.

Regions

Because many of modern Italy's 20 regions were independent states before unification, Italians often feel a greater allegiance to the town or region of their birth than to the country. San Marino, a tiny, independent state in northern Italy, managed to resist becoming part of united Italy. It claims to be the world's oldest republic, founded by Saint Marinus in the 4th century.

Italy's 20 regions

Mount Etna

Europe's only active volcanoes are in Italy. Mount Etna on Sicily (left) is one of the world's largest volcanoes. It stands over 3,200m high. It first erupted over two and a half million years ago. About 90 eruptions have been recorded since 1800 BC, and the most violent in 1669 AD swallowed 12 villages. Many people live in its shadow because the surrounding area is very fertile and rich in vineyards, olive groves and orchards.

Costa Smeralda

According to legend, the beautiful Costa Smeralda, or Emerald Coast, of Sardinia, is where the wind was born. Now, with its high cliffs and private coves, it is one of the world's most exclusive holiday regions. There are many rules to prevent the area being over-developed. All cables must run underground, for instance, and no building may rise above the tree tops. Costa Smeralda's picturesque marinas provide a haven for the yachts of the wealthy.

Wildlife & National parks

Although fewer people now live in the Italian countryside, human activities such as industrialisation, tree felling and hunting, have reduced the wildlife population. National parks have been established such as Stelvio and Abruzzi in the Dolomites to protect species such as the lynx, stoat, brown bear and golden eagle. Wolves and white mountain goats (right) still live in the mountains, and wild boar can be found, too.

13

CITIES AND TOWNS

More than two-thirds of Italy's population live in towns or cities. Rome, Milan, Naples and Turin are the largest cities. They are the centres of trade, industry and tourism. Italian cities tend to have an old historic centre. Most people live in modern apartment blocks on the outskirts. Most industry is also situated outside the city centre. Cities in the north tend to be more industrially advanced and prosperous than southern cities (see pages 28-29).

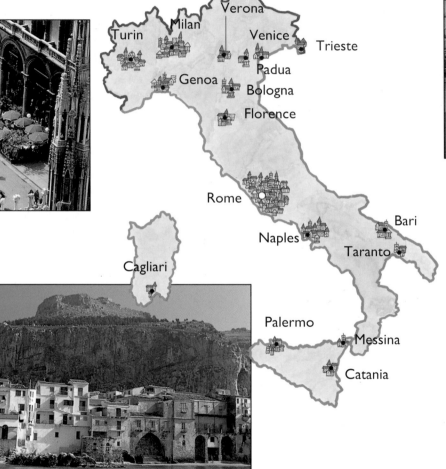

Milan is an industrial city, and the financial and commercial centre of Italy. *La Borsa* – Italy's stock exchange – is here. Its Gothic cathedral – *Il Duomo* – (above) can hold 40,000 worshippers.

Island towns such as Cefalu in Sicily (right) were once important centres of trade for the Phoenecians and the Romans. Today, tourism is the biggest industry.

Monument conservation
Italy earns huge sums from tourism, but it has to spend a fortune conserving and restoring its monuments. Natural wear and tear caused by the weather and centuries of tourism has been hastened by air pollution. Emissions from industry and motorvehicles have eaten away at marble and sandstone.

Leaning Tower of Pisa
Building began in 1173. Subsidence produced the lean when only three storeys were completed. The subsidence couldn't be stopped but building continued anyway. Recent work on the tower has reduced the 4.5 metre overhang by about 30cm. However, the lean is still considerable and the tower remains one of Italy's most popular attractions.

Market

Italians take their food very seriously, so buying the best quality ingredients is important. Italian markets sell a wide variety of high-quality food and most produce is local. In some areas, the stallholders sing the prices. Traditional markets are having to compete with modern supermarkets that sell convenience foods.

Many examples of modern architecture can be found in modern city centres such as Genoa (left). Some new buildings are spectacular and original.

Florence and the Golden Age

Success at war and the wool and silk trade made Florence the leading city in central Italy in the 13th century. Under the Medicis, a family of wealthy bankers, it became a centre of art and learning. During this Golden Age, Florence was home to some of the greatest artists of all time, such as the poets Dante and Petrarch, the painters Donatello, Botticelli and Michelangelo, and the sculptor Cellini. Leonardo Da Vinci trained as an artist in Florence. Today, tourists flock to the city to see the legacy of the great Renaissance artists.

Historic towns

Italy is rich in historic towns such as Venice, Siena, Florence and Genoa. During the Renaissance, these towns tried to outdo their neighbours with beautiful villas, palaces and churches. Today, many of these cities are centres of modern industry and commerce.

Preservation

Monuments such as the the Sistine chapel ceiling (right), in the Vatican City, need special attention. Preservation is an awkward subject. Mistakes have been made which worsened the state of some remains.

ROME

Once the heart of the Roman Empire, Rome was built on seven hills with the river Tiber running through its centre. It is a beautiful city, full of ancient monuments. When it was made the capital in 1871, Rome was neither Italy's largest nor most important city. But as the home of the Pope, whose palace is in the independent Vatican City, it has always been at the centre of the Roman Catholic Church. Today, Rome is at the heart of a problematic political system (see pages 20-21), but the Romans are proud of their city, and stand apart from the tensions between north and south.

Romulus and Remus
According to Roman myth, twins Romulus and Remus were thrown into the Tiber by their uncle. A she-wolf suckled them and a shepherd rescued them. They grew up to found Rome in 753 BC.

Remains of ancient Rome (left) can be seen throughout the city. Since the 1800s, the main sites of ruins have been surrounded with trees and gardens.

The Vatican
The Vatican City stands inside Rome. It became a separate country in 1929 and is the world's smallest state. It has been a papal residence since 1377 and is now the permanent home of the Pope. The Vatican City has a population of 1,000. The official language is Latin, and it is guarded by the Swiss Guard in their distinctive striped uniforms. Switzerland has provided a protective force for the papacy since the late 1400s. The present Pope, John Paul II, is from Poland. He is the first non-Italian Pope since 1542.

Villas and gardens

Rome's largest open space is the Villa Borghese, a collection of parks and gardens laid out in the grounds of a 17th-century palace, once owned by a wealthy family. It was bought for the public in 1902, and is a huge area of shady trees, lakes, grass and museums – an island of calm in a chaotic city. It includes the Galleria Borghese, one of Rome's finest picture galleries, which houses paintings by some of Italy's greatest painters such as Caravaggio, Raphael and Titian.

The Colosseum (above and left) stands in the centre of Rome. It was built in about 80 AD. It seated about 50,000 people who watched trained fighters who were called gladiators.

Old and new

The Pantheon and the Castel Sant Angelo (left) were built by the Romans and are still functioning buildings today. Roman ruins and medieval churches stand next to Renaissance palaces, baroque houses and modern office blocks. Mussolini promoted much badly planned construction, which has led to some of today's traffic problems.

World Cup fever

Football is taken very seriously in Italy, and when the country hosted the World Cup in 1990, many magnificent new stadia were built. Unfortunately, Italy, who have previously won the world cup three times, were beaten by Argentina in the semi-finals. The country has many impressive teams that perform well in European competitions. Rome alone has two top football clubs, Roma and Lazio, whose stadium is shown (right).

RURAL ITALY

The rural population in Italy is steadily declining. Since the end of World War II, millions of country people have moved to the northern cities in search of work (see pages 14-15). Most country people make their living from agriculture, cultivating small family farms or working in local vineyards. Every Italian village has a piazza, and usually a church, a municipo (town hall) and a police station. The only houses around the piazza belong to the village's wealthier inhabitants. Each village has at least one bar or café where villagers meet to talk and drink.

The Mafia
Originally, the Mafia or Cosa Nostra was a family-based secret society that protected communities threatened by invaders. In the 19th century, Sicilian landlords used the Mafia to control their estates and keep the peasants in order. Gradually, through intimidation, it won political and economic influence. Today, the Mafia is a violent organisation involved in organised crime such as drug trafficking, prostitution and extortion. It has spread its influence throughout Italian society, and has exported its terror abroad, especially to the United States (see page 10). Huge resources have been devoted to fighting the Mafia, but it is immensely powerful. The murders of anti-Mafia judges Falcone and Borsellino in 1993 clearly demonstrated the Mafia's capabilities.

Northern Italy
For centuries, people in the Alps have lived in small, isolated communities and made a living by farming or herding. After World War II land reclamation schemes in the Po valley and the Maremma plain have provided northern Italy with some of its richest agricultural areas.

Folklore
Each region has its own stories and traditions. La Befana is an ugly, but wise, old lady. At Epiphany (January 6), she leaves gifts for children in their socks if they've been good. In mountain areas there are many tales of werewolves, and some people wear a piece of coral in the shape of a horn to ward off the evil eye.

People

People's appearance reflects the country's geography and history. Many northern Italians are blond and Germanic in origin. In the south, which for centuries was occupied by Arabs and Spaniards, the people are much darker in appearance.

The elderly: old people are important and respected members of society in Italy.

The south

The south is known as the *Mezzogiorno*, meaning midday sun. It's mountainous, arris terrain is prone to earthquakes and it is one of the poorest areas in Europe, with 20% unemployment. Yet, the Italian government has recently allocated $50 billion to southern Italy, mainly for tourism infrastructure projects, to improve airports, railways

Religion

The majority of Italians are Roman Catholic, and the Church plays an important part in people's lives. However, the number of people who attend Mass regularly is decreasing and the Church's ability to influence politics has weakened since 1945.

Grave walls (above) are a common sight throughout Italy. Because of a shortage of land, instead of burying the dead in the ground, coffins are laid to rest in niches above ground. Graves are regularly tended by the family.

Cheese

Italian cheeses such as gorgonzola and parmesan are world famous. A mature parmesan is said to be so hard that it can stop a bullet. In Tuscany and Campania, buffalo milk is used to make mozzarella, which is used as a pizza topping. In mountainous regions, cheese is made from goat's milk.

ORGANISATION

Italy has been a republic since 1946, when King Umberto II abdicated following a referendum. The president is head of state and is elected for seven years and appoints the prime minister who forms the government. The president lives in the Quirinal Palace in Rome (right). The Italian parliament has two chambers – the Chamber of Deputies and the Senate. Since 1946, Italy has had over 50 governments, most of which have been coalitions led by the Christian Democrat party.

Monetary system

Up until 2002, the lira was Italy's currency, meaning "pound weight" in Latin. The lira has now been replaced by the euro, the new single currency to which most European nations belong. Italy's euro coins feature famous Italian works of art.

Police

There are two police forces in Italy, the Publicca Sicurezza, under the home secretary, and the Carabinieri, under the minister of defence. Both are responsible for investigating and preventing crime.

Abdication of the king

King Victor Emmanuel III abdicated in May 1946 after reigning for 46 years. His son, Umberto II, reigned for just one month, abdicating after 54 per cent of the people voted for a republic in a referendum. In 1947 Umberto II was exiled. The monarchy was unpopular because it had dragged Italy into World War II and supported the Fascists. Today, some Italians would like the monarchy restored.

Armed forces

The president is the supreme commander of the navy, air force and army, and has the power to declare war. Twelve to eighteen months of compulsory military service for all men over the age of 18 is in the process of being phased out so that it becomes a fully volunteer profession. At present, there are approximately 390,000 men and women in the armed forces, and Italy's military expenditure is one of the highest in the world.

Bombing of Bologna station
Italy's worst terrorist atrocity happened in 1980, when a bomb exploded at Bologna station (below), killing 85 people and injuring dozens more. Since World War II, Bologna has been the home of the Italian Communist Party, which made it a target for right-wing terrorists. After years of trials and appeals, a handful of people were imprisoned, although it was never proved who was ultimately behind the bombing, or what they hoped to achieve by it.

Parliament
The Senate (the upper chamber) has 315 elected members. The Chamber of Deputies (right) has 630 members, five of whom are elected for life. Both chambers have equal power when passing laws and general elections must be held at least every five years.

Local government
Italy has a *unitary* system of government which means central government has most of the power. Each of Italy's 20 regions has a representative in the Senate. However, each region is divided into provinces, which are made up of communes. Each region, province and commune has its own local council.

Judicial system
The highest court is the Constitutional Court, which can declare acts of parliament illegal. Of its 15 judges, five are chosen by the president, five by parliament and five by other Constitutional Court judges. Judges in other courts have to pass examinations before they are appointed. All courts, like the one on the right, come under the ministry of justice. Italian law is based on Roman law. Serious crime is heard at the court of assizes, and a number of lower courts deal with less serious cases.

EDUCATION AND LEISURE

Italian children must complete eight years of compulsory schooling, usually from six to 14. Italy's 47 public universities enrol over one million students a year; the largest, the University of Rome, enrols 120,000. Italy's mild climate makes outdoor sports and activities popular. Football is the most watched and played sport in Italy (see pages 16-17). Every major city has a football team. Skiing is also a popular sport and most ski resorts are in the Alps and Dolomites. Italians also enjoy going to cafés and restaurants and to the opera and cinema.

Education
Most children go to state schools. Only ten per cent attend private schools, often run by religious organisations. After five years of primary and three of secondary education, students go to technical college, teacher training school or prepare for the *Maturita*, the university entrance exam.

Sport
A relatively small percentage of Italians are actively involved in sport, yet Italy has produced a remarkable number of champions. They have particularly excelled in the fields of motor racing, cycling, basketball, athletics, skiing and football. Tennis and horse riding are both popular participant sports.

Italy has about 70 local daily newspapers. The most widely read newspapers are Turin's *La Stampa* and Rome's *La Repubblica*. *La Gazzetta* is a popular sports paper.

Movies
The Italians are passionate film-makers and film-goers. After World War II, Italian directors started making films on location instead of in studios. This gave their films a revolutionary style. In the 1960s, Italian-produced "Spaghetti" westerns became popular. Today, films such as *A Fistful of Dollars*, directed by an Italian, Sergio Leone (left),

Clint Eastwood (right) starred in *A Fistful of Dollars*.

Violin-making

Cremona was the birth place of the violin maker Antonio Stradivari (1644-1737). He made over a thousand violins, violas and cellos, which today are priceless. The city now has a school of violin-making.

Universities

Entry to university is automatic for all students that complete *Maturita*. The University of Bologna, founded in 1100, is one of the oldest in Europe. Today, it has 120,000 students. Florence (below) also has a large student population. It has a university, an academy of Fine Arts and the Luigi Cherubini conservatoire of music.

Festivals

Most festivals are dedicated to the Madonna or the local patron saint. Many festivals have pagan roots, like the procession in Cocullo, which bears aloft Saint Domenico's statue swathed in real snakes. There are festivals to celebrate every aspect of life. At Canelli, there is a festival to celebrate the hazelnut harvest. The Festival of St Elisio in Cagliari celebrates deliverance from plague in 1657. Florence holds a football match played in 16th-century costume to celebrate the fact that in 1530 the Florentines defiantly played football while the city was under siege.

Palio

The palio is a horse race around a square in Siena. Drums and flag throwers introduce the horses and jockeys in 15th-century costume who represent the city districts.

Venice

The Venice carnival lasts for ten days and ends on Shrove Tuesday. People go to balls in a mask, cloak and three-cornered hat.

Leisure

Hunting and fishing are popular pastimes. This dates back to Roman times, when every citizen was entitled to hunt. The one universal pastime in Italy is the evening *passeggiata*, when everyone takes to the streets for a stroll, to see and be seen.

AGRICULTURE AND FOOD

Agriculture employs ten per cent of the Italian workforce. Forty per cent of land is cultivated and most agricultural activity is in the south (see pages18-19). However, the Po valley in the north is the most intensively farmed region. It is Europe's biggest rice producer and Italy's principal area for livestock and dairy farming. Grapes are Italy's most valuable crop, while wheat and sugar beet are also important. Olives, tomatoes and citrus fruits are grown in the south. Fishing, though on a small scale, is the main source of income for many coastal areas.

Barley
Cattle
Dairy
Maize
Rice
Fruit
Pigs
Grapes
Wheat
Anchovies
Sardines
Wheat
Potatoes
Tobacco
Tuna
Olives
Sheep
Nuts
Citrus fruit

Wheat
The hard variety of wheat grown in the south is called durum wheat and is used for making pasta. The wheat grown in the north is soft and is used for making bread.

Fish
Most fish in Italy is imported, although the Mediterranean provides good catches of sardines, tuna and anchovies. Fish and seafood are especially popular in the south.

Livestock
Most cattle are raised in the north, and sheep and goats in central Italy, the south and Sardinia. Italy is short on pasture land, so a lot of meat has to be imported.

Wines

Italy is the world's largest wine producer, consumer and exporter. Every region produces its own wine. The stronger, heavier southern wines are often mixed to make vermouth or marsala. The best known wines – Soave, Barolo, Chianti and the fizzy Asti Spumante – are from the north. Wine is traditionally served with lunch and dinner.

Pasta

Pasta comes in over 200 shapes. Southern Italians eat tubular-shaped pasta and the northerners eat pasta ribbons. The names describe the pasta: spaghetti means "little string", vermicelli means "little worms".

Regional food

Italian food varies enormously from region to region, due to their independent pasts and differences in soil and climate. Polenta, a dish made from maize, comes from Lombardy. Risotto, made from rice, is a speciality of Milan. Pizza comes from Naples. Northern Italians tend to cook with butter, and southerners use extra virgin olive oil.

Olive oil

Italy is the world's biggest exporter of olives and olive oil. Olive groves are a common sight in central and southern Italy, as they grow well in the arid regions. The most commonly cultivated variety is the grey olive, from which the best olive oil is made. The oil is extracted by crushing the olives in presses. They can be pressed several times, although the oil from the first pressing, called virgin olive oil (below left), is the most prized by cooks. By the last pressing, the oil is inedible. This residue is called *olive foots* and is used in cosmetics, medicines, textiles and detergents. The olive tree lives longer than most fruit trees, and some olive trees, reputedly planted by Emperor Hadrian in 140 AD near Rome, are still alive.

Most regions produce their own cheeses (see page 19). Italy is famous for its sausages, salamis and cured meats such as parma ham (right).

Fishing ports

Italian waters are not well stocked with fish. Anchovies, sardines and tuna are the main catch. Apart from a few large fleets, fishing is still mainly an individual enterprise, and there are peaceful fishing ports dotted all around the coast, although many fishermen have left the industry.

INDUSTRY AND EXPORT

Since the Second World War, Italy's economy has changed from one based on agriculture into a ranking industrial one, producing clothing and shoes, food and drink, cars, machinery and chemicals. The industrial triangle formed by Milan, Turin and Genoa in northern Italy is one of the most advanced in Western Europe. One of the biggest problems facing Italian industry is the country's lack of natural fuel resources. Although it produces some natural gas, it has to import most of its fuel.

Marble

Italian marble is world renowned, especially the marble quarried at Carrara, which is so treasured by sculptors. This marble is translucent – light penetrates a short distance beneath the surface before it is reflected – which gives it a special glow. Marble has been quarried at Carrara since Roman times.

Italian sports cars

Italian sports cars such as Lamborghini, Bugatti and Ferrari are world famous for their style and power. Ferrari employs around 1,750 people and produces 2,400 hand-finished sports cars a year. Ferrari also has a Formula 1 racing team who won both the constructors' championship and the drivers' championship (with Michael Schumacher) in 2003.

Italian car industry

The Fiat company was established in Turin in 1899. Today, the company is a multinational organisation. The Lancia, Alfa Romeo and Ferrari trademarks also belong to Fiat. Fiat vehicles can be found the world over, from Eastern Europe to South America. Besides cars, Fiat manufactures buses, trucks and farm equipment, aircraft engines, trains and fire engines.

Textiles and clothes manufacture are two of Italy's most important industries. The wool and silk trade were the basis of Italy's prosperity in the Middle Ages, and they are still important today. Silk is still produced in Como, and Biella is famous for woollen cloth.

Glass-making

The Venetian island of Murano has been associated with glass-making since the 1200s. The Venetians led the world in glass-blowing techniques. They perfected *Cristallo* glass, which is colourless and transparent and can be blown very thinly and into any shape. Today, the city still makes some of the world's most beautiful glassware.

Alternative power

Because Italy has few natural fuel resources, it imports 75% of its energy requirements – mainly from the north African and Middle Eastern oil-producing nations. However, Italy has also developed its own alternative sources of power. Mountainous regions have been put to good use with the development of enormous hydroelectric projects, which produce a significant amount of energy. As a volcanic region, Italy is able to exploit geothermal power – this involves using the heat from beneath the Earth's surface to produce electricity. The most successful geothermal power stations are at Lardarello, near Florence.

Olivetti

The Olivetti office machinery company was founded by Camillo Olivetti in 1908 and made typewriters. Today, Olivetti is one of Europe's leading information technology companies, producing computers and office equipment. Olivetti employs over 30,000 people in 49 countries around the world. Olivetti products are renowned for their good design.

TODAY AND TOMORROW

Italy has developed a successful economy in spite of corruption and frequent changes of government. The north-south divide still remains a problem, the south remaining poor while northern Italians enjoy one of the highest standards of living in Europe. Recently, efforts have been made to address these problems, and the strength of the Mafia has been challenged (see pages 18-19). Italy continues to influence the rest of the world in automotive design and fashion. As a member of the G7 group of nations and the European Union, Italy has a substantial role to play in European politics.

The European Union
Under the Treaty of Maastricht, EU member countries have agreed to new levels of co-operation on money and social matters.

Flag of the European Union

The North Atlantic Treaty Organisation
NATO was established in 1950. Italy was one of the founders. The treaty stated that armed attack against a member in Europe or North America would be considered an attack against all members.

Flag of NATO

Italy's role in Europe

In the 1950s, Italy was a founding member of what was to become the European Union (EU). In 1999, Italian MP Romano Prodi became president of the European Commission. Today, Italians elect members to the European Parliament (above).

Political instability
Since World War II, Italy has suffered from a considerable degree of political instability. The proportional representation system has been partially responsible for the numerous changes in government, which has caused governments to be largely weak and ineffective. As a result, little has been done to reform the taxation system or reduce the national debt. Today, the political squabbles continue with the centre-left coalition, under Francesco Rutelli, challenging Silvio Berlusconi's centre-

right party. There are also extreme factions within the political framework, such as the right-wing Northern League. However, Italy has developed politically and is likely to continue doing so.

Tourism

As the world's fourth most popular holiday destination, tourism plays a vital part in the Italian economy. It is such a major industry that four per cent of the population work in it. Italy has attracted tourists and pilgrims from abroad for centuries. Today, Italy still attracts millions of pilgrims, but most people come for the skiing, the beaches, the museums and history, the food, the wine, and the sunshine.

Italy is a member of the **United Nations**, which it joined after World War II. The UN was set up to maintain peace and security and improve conditions in the member countries. Italian troops have been sent on various peace keeping missions around the world, including those in the Middle East, Somalia, and Mozambique.

Flag of the United Nations

North-south divide

The gap between wealthy northern Italy and the poor south has existed since unification. The most important reason for the gap is that the north is closer to Italy's trading partners and has more natural resources than the south. However, Mafia corruption, and emigration to the Americas in the 19th century, have also contributed. It is hoped that substantial government investment and EU funding in the south will reduce the divide.

Pollution

Industrial expansion and greater car ownership have caused terrible pollution, damaging monuments (see pages 14-15) and poisoning the seas and rivers. Efforts have been made to clean up the Bay of Naples and cars have been banned from some city centres. Venice (right) faces the possible effects of global warming. Rising sea levels threaten to leave it under water.

In the long term, efforts to stamp out corruption could lead to a political stability Italy has not experienced before. However, since World War II, Italy's economy has achieved a success that fifty years ago could not have been imagined.

FACTS AND FIGURES

Name: La Repubblica Italiana

Capital and largest city: Rome (population: 3,300,000)

Official language: Italian. Minorities of German, French and Slovenian speakers in the north, and Greek, Catalan and Albanian speakers in the south. In Sardinia, Sard is spoken.

Currency: As of 2002, the euro. Previously the lira

Population: 57,998,000

Population density: 192 persons per km^2

Distribution: 67 % in urban areas, 33% in rural areas.

Ethnic groups: mostly Italian

Major religions: Roman Catholic 82%, nonreligious 14%, Muslim 1%, other 3%.

Area: 301,268km^2. Max distance east-west 515km, north-south 1,139km

Highest mountain: Mont Blanc, 4,807m

Coastline: 7,600km

Main rivers: Po, Tiber, Arno, Brenta and Adige.

Climate: Warm, temperate and Mediterranean in the south, with mild winters. The north has hot, dry summers and cold winters. The Adriatic coast is subject to north-east winds such as the Bora.

AVERAGE JANUARY TEMPERATURES

- Above 5
- 4-8
- 0-4
- Below 0

Degrees Celsius

AVERAGE JULY TEMPERATURES

- Above 24
- 20-24
- 16-20
- Below 16

Degrees Celsius

ANNUAL RAINFALL

- Over 150
- 100-150
- 75-100
- Below 75

Centimetres

Physical features: Along Italy's northern border, the Alps stretch east-west. The Apennines occupy the centre of Italy's peninsula, running almost the entire length of the country. The Po river valley is Italy's only major flat area.

Borders: Italy is surrounded by the Tyrrhenian, Adriatic, Ligurian and Ionian seas. Italy borders Switzerland, Slovenia, Austria and France.

AGRICULTURE

Land use: Forests and woodland 32%, arable land 30%, permanent pastures 21%, permanent crops 9%, other 8%.

Crop production 2003: (tonnes) Maize 9.7 million, sugar beet 8.3 million, grapes 8 million, tomatoes 6.8 million, wheat 6.3 million, olives 3.1 million, potatoes 1.8 million, apples 2 million, oranges 2 million, peaches and nectarines 1.3 million, rice 1.3 million, barley 1 million.

Fisheries: total catch (in 2003) 609,768 tonnes.

Livestock: Chickens 130 million, goats 13.7 million, sheep 10.5 million, pigs 7.7 million, cattle 7 million.

Mineral resources

Italy is poor in mineral resources with only marble, granite, mercury (accounting for around 25 per cent of world production) and sulphur being produced in sufficient quantities for export.

Industry

Textiles, motor vehicles, machinery, fashion, iron and steel, electronics. Other important industries include glass, leather goods, food processing and marble.

Imports

Chemicals 16%, machinery and transport equipment 11%, metal 10%, food 6%, petroleum 4%, textiles 4%.

Major import sources:

Germany 17.8%, France 11.3%, Netherlands 5.9%, U.K. 5%, U.S. 4.9%, Spain 4.6%.

Exports

Machinery and transport equipment 42%, chemicals 10%, textiles 8%, clothing (including shoes at 3%) 7%, metal and processed metal 7%.

Major export destinations:

Germany 13.7%, France 12.2%, U.S. 9.8%, U.K. 6.9%.

ELECTRICITY

Production by source:

Fossil fuels:	78.6%
Hydroelectric:	18.4%
Other:	3%

ECONOMY

The GDP (gross domestic product) is the amount of goods and services produced within a country. By dividing the GDP by the population a *per capita* result is reached.

Figures shown are the GDP per capita in the year 2002. (GDPs are shown in U.S. dollars).

Italy	24,915
U.S.	35,935
Belgium	28,964
Netherlands	27,011
Germany	26,234
U.K.	25,427
Spain	20,660

Italy is one of the founder members of the European Union, signing the Treaty of Rome in 1957. The six original members were Italy, France, Germany, the Netherlands, Belgium and Luxembourg. The EU is committed to achieving closer economic and political ties between its members and can pass laws governing many aspects of administration, such as agriculture, the environment and health. In 2004, another ten countries joined the EU. They were Cyprus, the Czech Republic, Estonia, Hungary, Latvia, Lithuania, Malta, Poland, Slovakia and Slovenia.

FAMOUS FACES

LITERATURE

Virgil (70 BC-19 BC).
See page 11.

Dante Alighieri
(1265-1321, right).
Dante's most famous work is *The Divine Comedy*, in which he journeys through Hell, Purgatory and Paradise. By writing in Italian, he showed it could be as expressive and sophisticated as Latin.

Francesco Petrarca (1304-74).
Known in English as Petrarch, he was one of the earliest modern lyric poets. He is best known for a series of love poems called *Canzoniere*.

Nicoló Machiavelli (1469-1527, left).
See page 11.

Giuseppe di Lampedusa (1896-1957).
Son of the Duke of Parma, Lampedusa's once rich family wasted its wealth. He wrote just one novel, *The Leopard* (1958), set in 19th-century Sicily. It is widely recognised as the greatest 20th-century Italian novel.

Umberto Eco (1932-).
Eco achieved international fame with his best-selling novel *The Name of the Rose* (1980).

MUSICIANS

Antonio Vivaldi (1678-1741).
A Venetian violinist and composer, Vivaldi was known as the Red Priest, because of his red hair. Although his music was forgotten after his death, in the 20th century his music was rediscovered. His *Four Seasons* (1725) has grown in popularity and become one of the most widely enjoyed pieces of classical music.

Nicoló Paganini (1782-1840, left).
The son of a Genoese porter, Paganini was a child prodigy on the violin. As an adult, his dexterity and brilliance caused a sensation throughout Europe, and it was said his talent came from being in league with the devil. He revolutionised violin technique.

Giuseppe Verdi (1813-1901, right).
The son of an inn-keeper, Verdi's ambition was to be a cathedral organist. After the death of his wife and children, his career rocketed. Operas like *Rigoletto* (1851), *La Traviata* (1853) and *Otello* (1887) made him the leading operatic composer of the day, although he remained a simple countryman. Verdi's works are performed today more than those of any other composer.

Enrico Caruso (1873-1921, right).
A Neapolitan, Caruso's vocal power and purity, together with his great acting ability, have earned him the reputation as one of the great operatic tenors of all time.

Arturo Toscanini (1867-1957).
Toscanini won a scholarship to study music at the age of nine. He became a leading conductor, and worked for many years at La Scala, the Metropolitan Opera House in New York, and Bayreuth in Germany. His attention to detail earned him a reputation as a tyrant.

ARTISTS

Donato Bramante (1444-1514).
Bramante started as a painter, before becoming an architect. He worked in Milan and Rome, for Popes Alexander VI and Julius II, and designed the basilica of St. Peter's, Rome.

Leonardo da Vinci
(1452-1519, right).
One of the three greatest artists of the Renaissance. His painting, sculpture and architecture are renowned, but he was also a poet, musician, inventor and scientist. *La Giaconda* (Mona Lisa) is his most famous painting.

Michelangelo Buonarroti (Michelangelo) (1475-1564, left).
Worked as a painter, sculptor and poet. Among his greatest works are the Sistine Chapel ceiling and the design for the dome of St. Peter's cathedral in Rome.

Tizianio Vecellio (Titian) (1477-1576).
Titian was the greatest of the Venetian painters and has been described as the founder of modern painting. He painted many mythical and religious pictures, together with a number of portraits of emperors and popes.

Michelangelo da Caravaggio
(1573-1610, right).
Caravaggio was perhaps the greatest Italian painter of the 17th century. His works are intensely dramatic, with realistic figures emerging from dark shadow. He often used passers-by as models for biblical characters. He fled Rome after killing a man, and lived the rest of his life as a refugee.

Giovanni Antonio Canal (Canaletto) (1697-1768).
Canaletto lived most of his life in Venice, although he spent ten years in England. On returning to Italy, his views of the city became immensely popular and made him very rich. Many of his views of Venice are little changed today.

Amedeo Modigliani (1884-1920).
A painter and sculptor, Modigliani's early work was influenced by Renaissance painters. After moving to Paris, he turned to sculpture, which influenced his later elongated portraits, noted for their rich colour. Only after his death from tuberculosis did he gain recognition.

SCIENTISTS & EXPLORERS

Giovanni Caboto (1450-1498).
Giovanni Caboto, known as John Cabot in English, was commissioned by Henry VII of England to discover unknown lands. He became the first European to touch the North American mainland, although he thought he was in north-east Asia. He sailed again in 1498, touching Greenland, and probably died on the voyage.

Enrico Fermi (1901-1954, above).
After winning the 1938 Nobel Prize for physics, Enrico Fermi went from the prize ceremony in Stockholm straight to the United States, fearful for the safety of his Jewish wife in Italy. He played an important role in atomic research, and the element fermium was named after him.

Guglielmo Marconi (1874-1937, left).
The son of an Italian father and Irish mother, Marconi made his first successful wireless telegraphy experiments in 1895. In 1898, he transmitted signals across the English Channel, and across the Atlantic in 1901. His work won him the 1909 Nobel Prize for physics.

HISTORICAL FIGURES

Augustus Caesar (63 BC-14 AD, right).
After the death of Julius Caesar, Augustus outmaneuvered or defeated his rivals, including Mark Anthony and Cleopatra. He became sole ruler of the Roman world in 31 BC after the battle of Actium, and became emperor in 27 BC. He reformed the law, government and the army, beautified Rome and expanded the Empire.

Lorenzo "the Magnificent" de' Medici (1449-1492, left).
Lorenzo became ruler of Florence in 1469, and turned it into the leading state in Italy. He courageously thwarted attempts to wrest power from him, and his generous and enthusiastic patronage of the arts cemented Florence's glorious reputation.

Girolamo Savonarola (1452-1498, right).
A political and religious reformer, Savonarola cleverly took control of Florence when it became a republic in 1493. He stamped out all frivolity, and Florentines were obliged to cast all fancy clothing and ornaments on to the public "bonfires of vanities". He was excommunicated for claiming to be a prophet, and was eventually tortured and hanged by the Church for his beliefs.

Giacomo Casanova (1725-1798).
An Italian adventurer, Casanova is most famous for his romantic escapades. By the age of 25 he had been a cardinal's secretary, a soldier, a gambler, an alchemist and a violinist, and in 1756 made a daring escape from prison. He travelled throughout Europe, and was director of state lotteries in Paris, was knighted in the Netherlands, fled Russia after a duel, and worked as a spy. His memoirs detail his amorous conquests.

Giuseppe Mazzini (1805-72, right).
Mazzini prepared the ground for Italian unity, by writing and agitating tirelessly, mainly from exile. He participated enthusiastically in the 1848 uprisings and supported Garibaldi in his campaigns in Sicily and Naples.

THE ITALIAN LANGUAGE

Italian is the first language of about 60 million people. It is one of Switzerland's official languages. Because of its Latin origins it is called a Romance language, as are Portuguese, French, Spanish and Romanian, which have many similarities with Italian. The English language has borrowed and adapted many Italian words such as balcony, carnival, umbrella, costume, granite, laundry, malaria and volcano. Much of the vocabulary of music is Italian: piano, opera, cello, glissando, concerto and allegro, for example. As traders and bankers, the Italians also developed early accounting methods, and words such as cash and bankrupt come from Italian.

Other Italian words used in English:

mafia	organised crime
pilot	aircraft controller
stucco	light plaster
al fresco	outside
al dente	to the tooth
coda	end (in music)
presto	quickly
pronto	ready
ciao	hello / goodbye

INDEX

Photocredits

Abbreviations: l-left, r-right, b-bottom, t-top, c-centre, m-middle
Front cover both, back cover — Digital Stock. Cover tr, 1, 2b, 4m, 4b, 6ml, 7br, 8tl, 10tl, 10-11, 11t, 12ml, 12-13, 14t, 14-15, 15t, 15ml, 16t, 16mr, 16-17, 17t, 17ml, 18t, 18m, 19br, 20tl, 20r, 21tl, 21r, 21b, 22c, 24t, 24mr, 24ml, 24br, 25ml, 25m, 26tl, 26r, 26mr, 26b, 26-27, 27t, 29mt, 29bl — Select Pictures. 2mr, 11bl, 19bl, 20ml, 22ml, 25tl, 25r, 25b — Roger Vlitos. 2tl, 5, 7bl, 13bl, 14m, 14b, 15mr, 16ml — Italian State Tourist Office (ENIT), London. 3, 10ml, 10m, 12t, 12mr, 12b, 13m, 15br, 19t, 23mr, 23bl, 23r, 25mr, 29br — Emma Price Thomas. 4-5, 17mr — Spectrum Colour Library. 6b, 11br, 15bl, 17b, 18b, 21m, 22mr, 22b, 26ml, 28br, 31 — Frank Spooner Pictures. 8m, 9 all, 20b — Hulton Deutsch. 10mr, 27b — Olivetti. 11m — First One Moltini. 19m, 24bl — Eye Ubiquitous. 20r — PBD. 22tl — Brian Hunter Smart. 23ml — Robert Harding Picture Library. 27m — Fiat. 28t — Sportsfoto. 28ml — Universal Pictorial Press & Agency Ltd. 29trt, 29trm — Digital Stock. 29trb — Corbis.